D0264860

MY
WORLD
OF
ANIMALS

MY WORLD OF ANIMALS

Illustrated by Doreen McGuinness
Written by Angela Sayer Rixon

DEAN

This compilation first published 1994 by Dean, an imprint of
Reed Children's Books , Michelin House, 81 Fulham Road,
London SW3 6RB, and Auckland, Melbourne, Singapore and Toronto.

Text copyright © 1990, 1992, 1994 Reed International Books Limited.
Illustrations pages 2, 10-21, 32-39, 50-61, 72-75, 78-81, 88-91, 92-95 and
various cover illustrations copyright © 1990, 1994 Doreen McGuinness.
Doreen McGuinness is represented by Garden Studios, London.
All other illustrations copyright © 1992, 1994 Reed International Books Limited.

All rights reserved. No part of this publication may be reproduced, stored in a
retrieval system, or transmitted, in any form, or by any means, electronic,
mechanical, photocopying, recording or otherwise, without the prior
permission of the copyright holders.

ISBN 0 603 55414 8

British Library Cataloguing-in-Publication Data.
A catalogue record for this book is available from the British Library.

Printed in France
by Pollina, 85400 Luçon - n° 65598

CONTENTS

Animals in our homes

cat

guinea pig

rabbit

goldfish

budgerigar

dog

Pets and their babies

Baby cats are called kittens. They are born with their eyes closed, but after about a week they open them.

Mother rabbits make soft nests of hay and fur for their babies. The babies are born without any fur and with their eyes closed. As they grow older, fur grows on their bodies and their eyes open.

Baby dogs are called puppies. Their mother looks after them while they are young. She feeds them with her milk and licks them clean with her wet tongue.

Animal families of parks and gardens

wagtail

moorhen

cuckoo

deer

swan

grebe

11

Swans and cuckoos

A mother swan usually lays about six eggs in her nest.
The nest is made of water plants and twigs. When the eggs
hatch, the baby swans appear. They are called cygnets and have
fluffy grey feathers. They can swim well, but stay close to their
parents. Their mother pulls up water plants for them to eat.

The cuckoo lays her eggs in the
nests of other birds. First she watches
a bird build its nest and lay an egg. Then
she waits until it leaves. Quickly she throws out
the egg, lays one of her own and flies away. Soon
the other bird comes back. She thinks the egg is hers.
When the cuckoo hatches, she looks after it until it can fly.

Animal families of ponds and rivers

warbler

damselfly

toad

stickleback

water spider

water snail

14

bittern

frog

water shrew

15

Beginning life under water

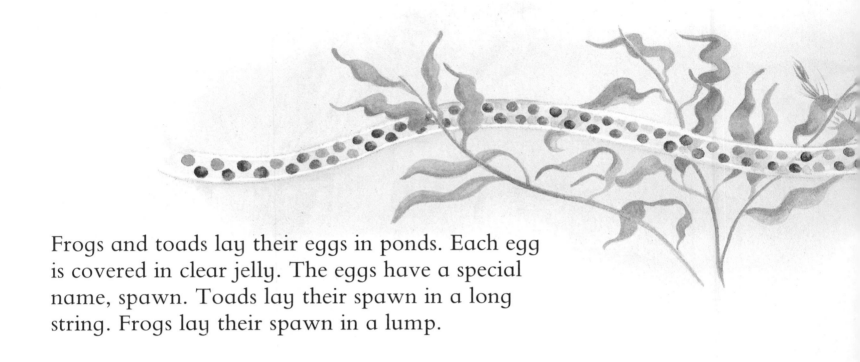

Frogs and toads lay their eggs in ponds. Each egg is covered in clear jelly. The eggs have a special name, spawn. Toads lay their spawn in a long string. Frogs lay their spawn in a lump.

Each egg hatches into a tadpole. The tadpole grows back legs. Then the tail slowly disappears and the front legs grow.

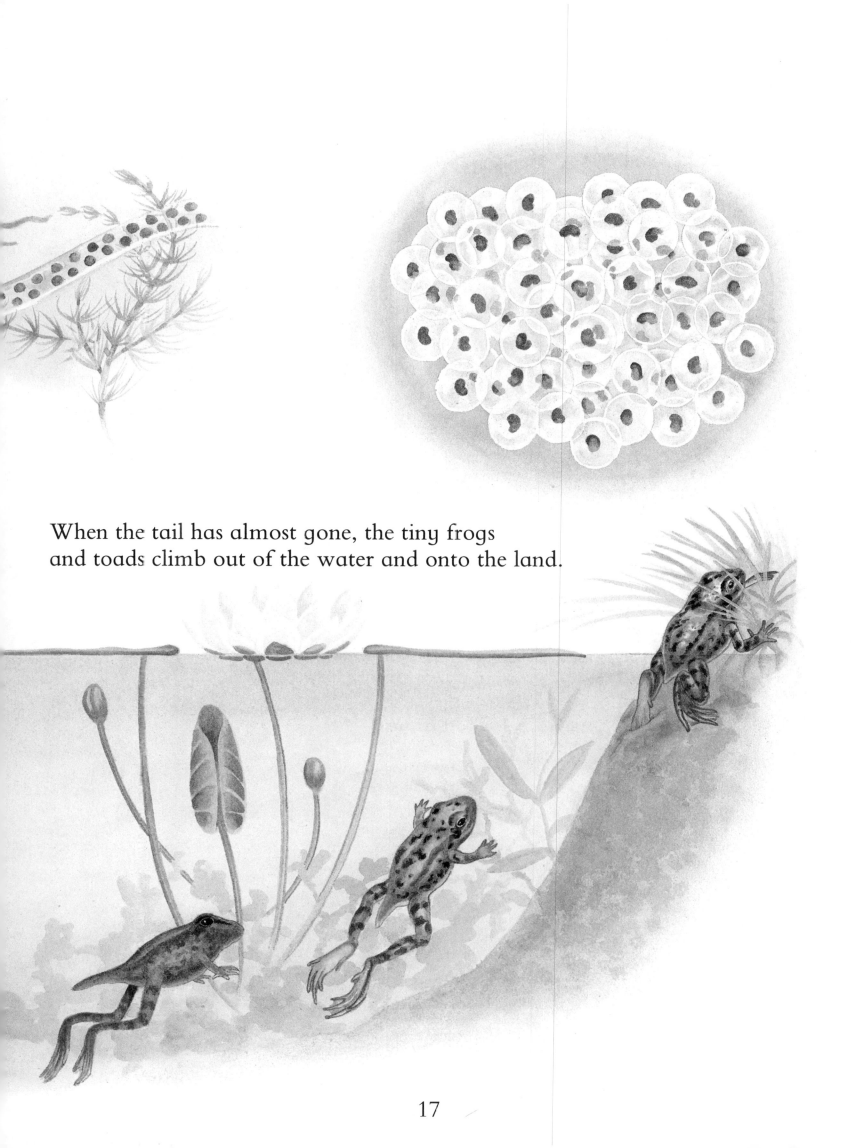

When the tail has almost gone, the tiny frogs
and toads climb out of the water and onto the land.

Animal families of cold woods and forests

grey squirrel

wood mouse

slow-worm

redstart

jay

butterfly

ladybird

moth

19

Butterflies and moths

Butterflies and moths lay their eggs on plant leaves. The mother chooses a plant that her babies will like to eat.

When the caterpillar is fully grown, it turns into a chrysalis. Inside the hard shell of the chrysalis, wings grow and many other changes happen.

Tiny caterpillars hatch from the eggs. Each one looks like a small, coloured worm.

The caterpillars feed on the plants and grow. But their skin does not grow with them. Each time it gets too small, it splits and falls off. Underneath is a new, bigger skin.

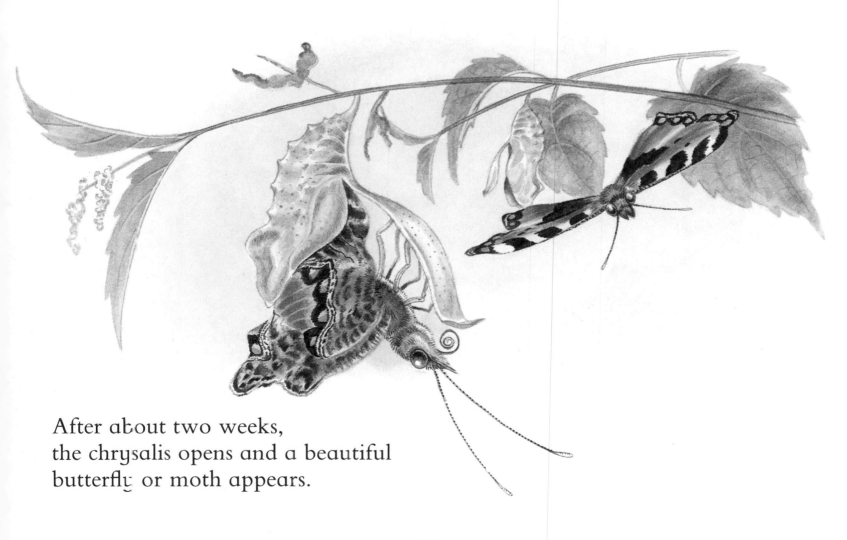

After about two weeks, the chrysalis opens and a beautiful butterfly or moth appears.

Building a home

Beavers have large, strong teeth. They use them to gnaw through tree trunks. They use the tree trunks to build dams across rivers. Behind the dams, the beavers make large nests of sticks, stones and mud, called lodges.

Coots hide their nests in reeds in the middle of rivers. The nests are made from dead leaves. In their nests, coots lay at least four eggs.

22

Water voles build their homes in river banks.
First they make a hole in the bank, then they
dig long tunnels through the earth. In the
middle of the tunnels, the voles make nests
lined with grass.

Animals of fields and hedgerows

pheasant

hare

mole

adder

dormouse

hedgehog

stoat

Sleeping through the winter

The hedgehog eats slugs, snails and insects.
These are hard to find in the winter. So,
when the cold weather starts, the hedgehog
makes a warm, cosy bed of dry leaves.
It crawls into the bed and curls up into a
tight ball. Then it sleeps until the weather
gets warm again.

The dormouse is another little animal
which sleeps through the winter.
It builds itself a nest with dry leaves
and strips of bark. Then it wraps its
tail around its body and goes to
sleep until spring.

When the cold weather comes, the adder finds a deep,
warm hole. It crawls inside and coils itself round and round.
When it wakes up in the spring, it shakes off its old skin.
Underneath it has a shiny new skin.

Animals on the farm

cow

sheep

pig

chicken

horse

turkey

duck

29

Farm animals which help us

Many farm animals help us.

Cows give us milk. The farmer milks them with a machine.
Later, a lorry takes the milk to a dairy. There, some milk is
made into butter and cheese. The rest is put into bottles
or cartons for people to buy.

Chickens give us eggs. Each chicken lays
an egg every day. The farmer collects the
eggs and keeps some for his family.
The other eggs are packed into boxes
and sent to shops.

Sheep give us wool. They grow
thick coats of wool to keep warm
in the winter. When the spring
comes, the farmer cuts off the
thick wool. This is called
shearing. The wool is
taken to a factory. There it is
washed, spun and dyed many
bright colours.

31

Animal families of the clifftops

gannet

peregrine falcon

cormorant

puffin

razorbill

albatross

33

Seabird babies

The razorbill lays one egg on a rock ledge on the top of a cliff. The egg is pear-shaped so that it cannot roll off. Each parent has two bare patches under its body. The parents take it in turns to sit on the egg and always make sure that it is under the patches. This keeps the egg very warm until the chick comes out.

The gannet also keeps its egg under its body. The parents take it in turns to look after the egg. They use their large feet to wrap around it and keep it warm.

Puffins make burrows to use as nests. They dig them with their heavy beaks and scrape away the mud with their feet. The nest is lined with grass and feathers and the mother puffin lays one egg in it. After six weeks the baby puffin hatches. It stays in the burrow so that gulls cannot attack it.

Animal families of the oceans

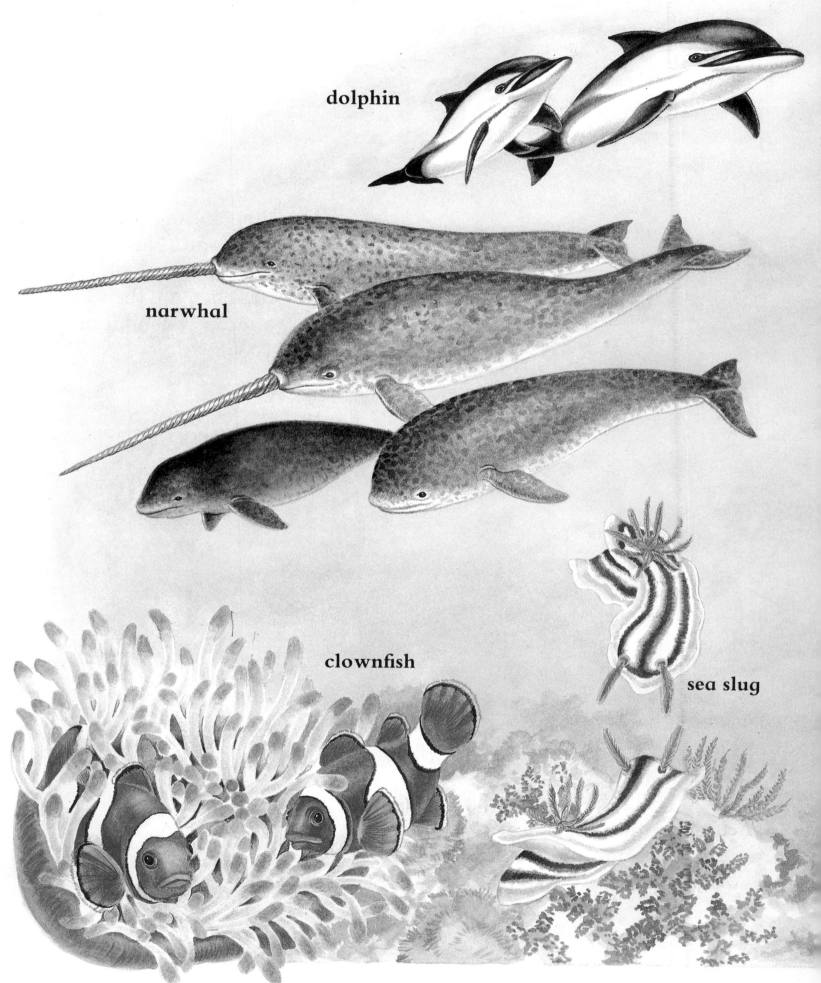

dolphin

narwhal

clownfish

sea slug

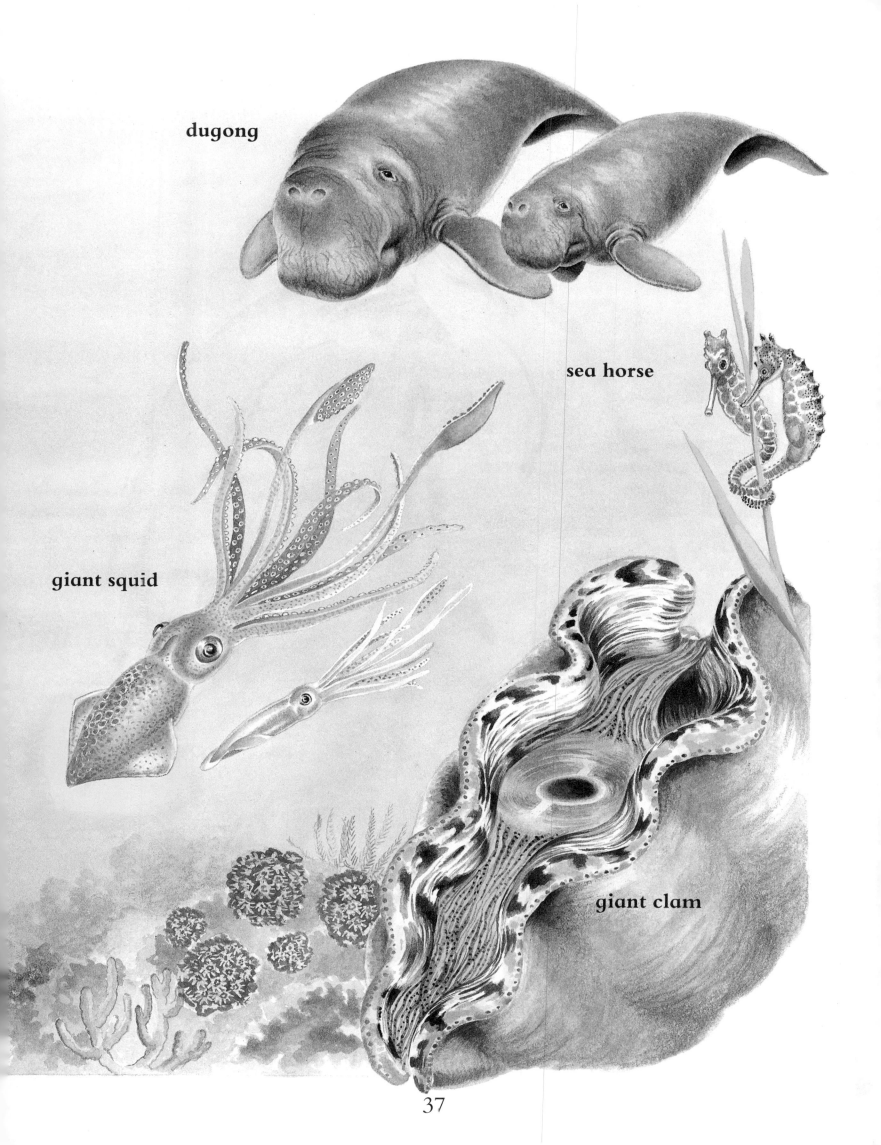

dugong

sea horse

giant squid

giant clam

Coming up for air

A baby dolphin is called a calf. As soon as a calf is born
it must breathe air. The mother dolphin pushes it to the surface
of the water with her snout. Sometimes dolphin "aunts" help her.
On the surface, the calf breathes and drinks milk from its mother.

The mother seahorse lays her eggs into a special pouch on the father's body. After about four weeks, the eggs hatch. One by one the tiny baby seahorses pop out of the pouch. Then they float to the surface of the water to gulp air. Seahorses keep this air in a special place rather like a pouch inside their bodies. It weighs them down in the water and helps them to swim with their heads up.

Sea animals in danger

Dolphins are small whales. They live in large groups called schools. Dolphins are very clever animals and can be trained to do tricks.

Whales live in the sea, but they breathe air just like people. They can dive under water and stay there for about an hour. Then they must come up to the top to get air again.

Tiny coral animals live together in large groups under the sea. There they grow hard shells around themselves which join up to make reefs. The shells grow in many beautiful colours.

There are not many of these animals left in the world. Now people are trying to protect them so that they do not die out altogether.

Animals of ice and snow

polar bear

musk ox

arctic fox

arctic hare

snowy owl

penguin

ptarmigan

lemming

reindeer

43

On the move

Reindeer live in ice and snow for most of the
year. They have special feet which help them
walk on snow and dig up plants to eat. In
the winter, reindeer go on a long journey to
warmer places. There they can still find food.
They go back to the snow in the spring.

Lemmings are small, furry animals a bit like
mice. They make their homes in tunnels
under the snow, but they do not always stay
there. Sometimes they leave because they
need to find food. Sometimes they leave
because they have so many babies that there
is not enough room for them all.

Musk oxen also live in the snow. They have a thick coat
of long hair to keep them warm. When the winter comes,
they join together in large groups called herds.
Then, like the reindeer, they walk a very long way to
places where they can still find grass and plants to eat.

Animals of the mountains

condor

cougar

llama

ibex

red panda

giant panda

yak

Pandas

Two rare animals live in the mountains of China.
They are both types of panda, but they look quite
different from one another.

The red panda is sometimes called a cat-bear,
because it looks rather like a cat. It spends most
of the day in trees, but climbs down at night
and eats fruit, leaves, seeds and birds' eggs.

Giant pandas live in high forests. They are shy and spend most of their time on their own. Their main food is a hard type of grass called bamboo, but they do eat other plants, too. These pandas sometimes climb trees, but usually live on the ground.

Animal families of the Antarctic

emperor penguin

adelie penguin

snow petrel

great skua

macaroni penguin

51

Penguins and their chicks

A mother emperor penguin lays a single egg.
After a few days she passes it to the father.
Then she goes to eat fish in the sea.

The father penguin stands with the egg on
his feet. He covers it with a special fold of
skin to keep it warm. He stays in the same
place for two months and does not eat.

In the spring, the egg hatches. The mother
comes back to look after her chick. Then the
father can go to find food.

Adelie penguins make their nest with stones. The mother lays two eggs in it. Then both parents take turns to keep the eggs warm.

When the chicks are born they are grey and fluffy. After four weeks they leave the nest and join many other chicks on the seashore. When they are fully grown, their parents take them down to the sea. There they learn to catch their own food.

Animal families of the American forests

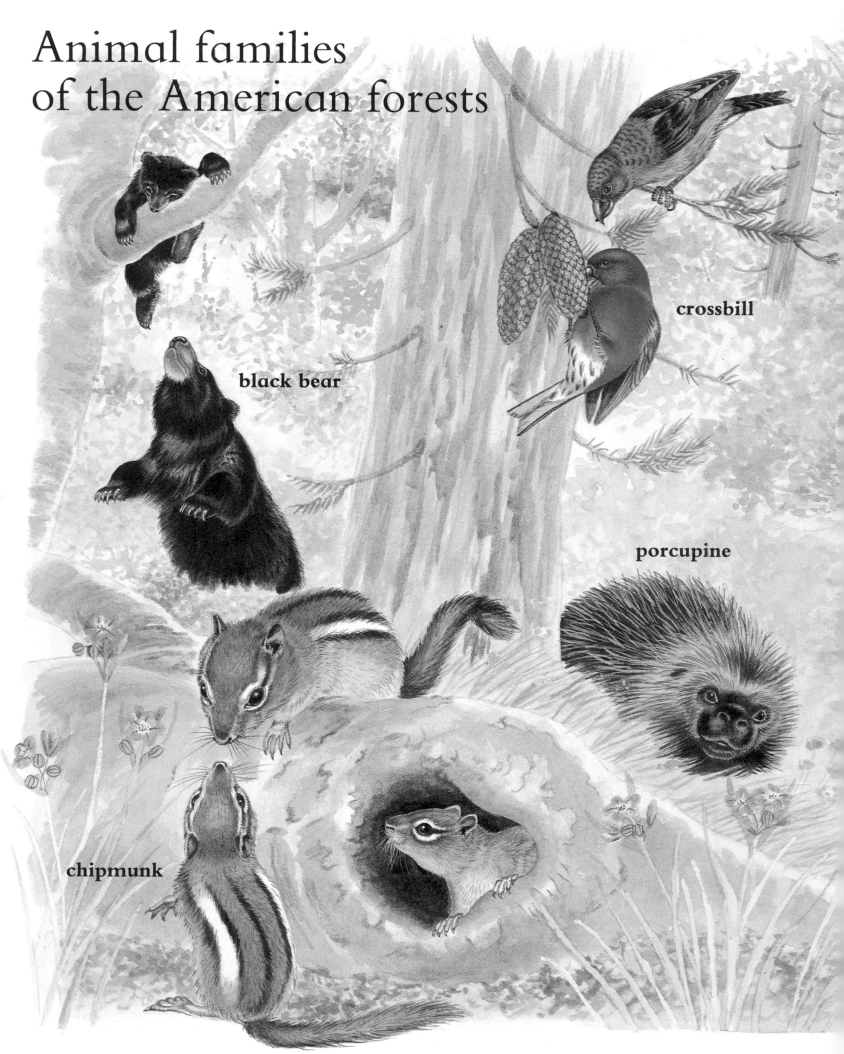

black bear

crossbill

porcupine

chipmunk

raccoon

screech owl

bobcat

moose

Raccoons and porcupines

A raccoon mother usually has three or four babies at a time. She takes care of them without any help from the father raccoon. After ten weeks, the babies can leave the nest. Then they join their mother on her night trips to find food. The babies and their mother growl and purr so that they do not lose one another in the dark.

Porcupines usually have only one baby at a time. The babies are born with long black hair and short spines, called quills. They can see and walk straightaway. After two days, they can even climb trees!

Animal families of the American deserts

elf owl

gila woodpecker

cactus wren

roadrunner

gila monster

American badger

kit fox

rattlesnake

desert tortoise

59

Keeping safe and cool

Elf owls are very, very small. They make their nests inside holes high up in giant cacti. Sometimes they use holes that gila woodpeckers have made and left behind. The prickles of the cacti help to protect the nests from danger.

Roadrunners lay their eggs in nests in desert
bushes. They have to protect the eggs from
the hot sun. To do this, the mother and father
sit on them in turn. Roadrunner chicks are
born with only a few black feathers. Their
parents must shade them from the great heat
of the desert until they are fully grown.

61

Animals of grasslands and prairies

pronghorn

coyote

gopher

eagle

bison

prairie dog

kangaroo rat

Underground homes

The prairie dog is really a kind of squirrel. It lives underground with its family in a prairie dog "town". When the family goes above ground to find food, one prairie dog stands guard at the entrance to their tunnel.

Gophers also live in underground tunnels,
but each gopher lives alone. A gopher's
home has two tunnels, one underneath the
other. The top tunnel is where the gopher
finds roots and shoots to eat. The lower
tunnel is where it lives and sleeps.

Animals of the deserts

jack rabbit

lizard

coral snake

falcon

camel

scorpion

fennec fox

Camels

There are two types of camel. Arabian camels live in hot deserts. They have short hair so that they do not get too hot. Bactrian camels live in cold deserts. They have long hair to keep them warm.

All camels have lumps on their back called humps. Arabian camels have one hump and Bactrian camels have two humps. The humps have fat in them. The camels use this as food on their long journeys across the desert.

All camels also have special feet to help them walk in the desert. Each foot has two toes joined by a piece of skin. When a camel walks, the skin spreads out. This stops the camel from sinking in the sand.

Animals of the African plains

hippopotamus

African elephant

zebra

giraffe

cheetah

ostrich

lion

baboon

rhinoceros

71

Animal families of the African plains

zebra

cheetah

antelope

ostrich

lion

mongoose

73

Hiding in the grass

Cheetahs and lions eat zebras. They chase them through the long grass of the plains. Young zebras are called foals. They cannot run very fast and so are always in danger. Luckily they are born with brown fur over their striped coats. This helps them to hide until they are strong enough to run fast.

Cheetah cubs are sometimes in danger, too, because lions and hyenas eat them. A mother cheetah often has to leave her cubs alone while she hunts for food. The cubs have dark

74

fur under their bodies and long, grey hairs over their heads and necks. This covering is called a mantle. It helps the little cheetahs to hide from danger.

Biggest and fastest

Elephants are the biggest land animals in
the world. They roam around in family
groups called herds. Elephants live in hot
countries, so they need to keep cool. To do
this, they spray water over one another with
their trunks.

The cheetah can run faster than any other animal in the world. It needs to run fast to catch animals and birds to eat. Cheetahs hunt for their food early in the morning. They rest later in the day when the sun gets very hot.

Animal families
of the African woodlands

flying squirrel

hornbill

chimpanzee

grey parrot

weaver bird

okapi

black
mamba

elephant shrew

79

Unusual nests

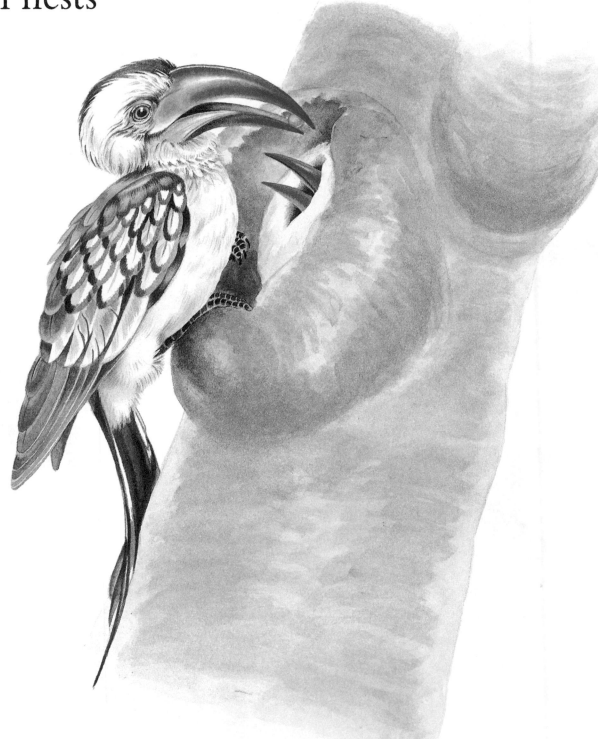

The hornbill lays her eggs in a hole inside a
tree. Then she blocks up the hole from the
inside. She leaves just a narrow slit open.
The father feeds the mother through this slit.
When the chicks hatch, he brings food for
the whole family. The chicks grow quickly
and soon have all their feathers. Finally the
mother hornbill breaks out of the hole. Then
the chicks can leave the nest and learn to fly.

The father weaver bird builds the nest for his family. First he pulls off a long strip of grass. Then he loops the strip over a branch and joins the ends. He repeats this many times and weaves all the strips together. The nest looks like a round basket with a small opening. When it is ready, the mother weaver bird goes inside and lays her eggs.

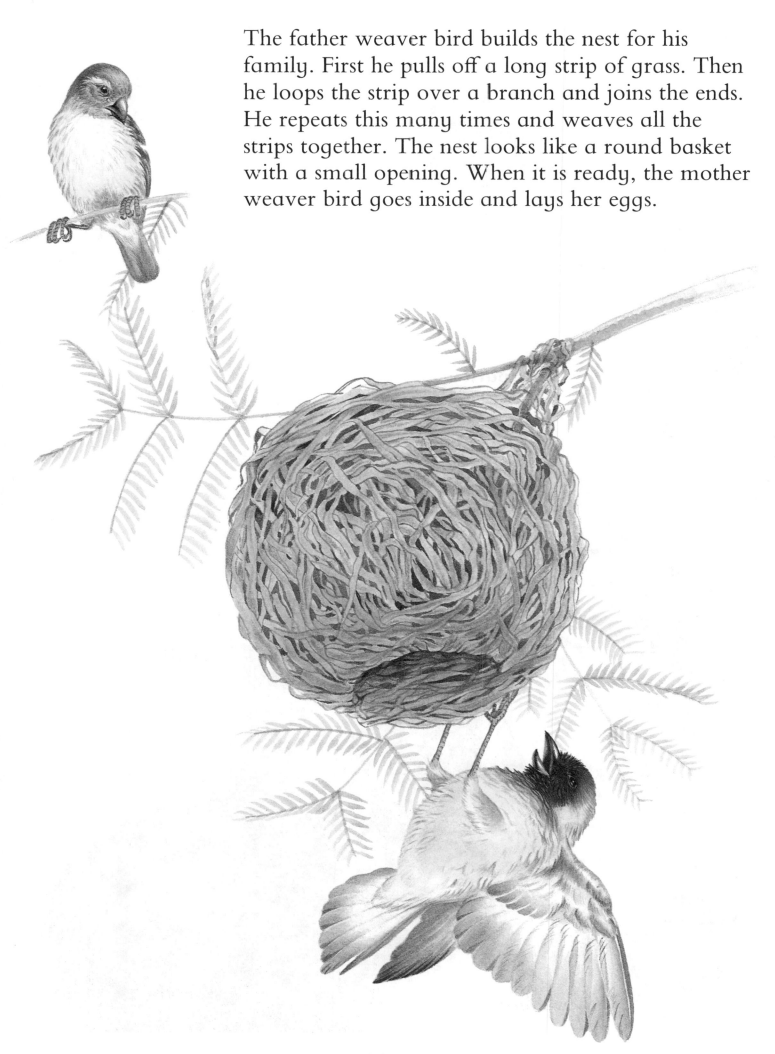

Animals of the rainforests

leopard

monkey

tree frog

gorilla

bushbaby

fruit bat

python

parrot

tiger

Rainforest animals at night

The leopard is a big, spotted cat. It is very
good at climbing, running and swimming.
In the daytime it sleeps quietly in the sun,
usually in a tree. At night it hunts for food.

Fruit bats wake up when it starts to get dark. Then they fly off to find figs and other fruit to eat. In the morning they fly back to their tree. Then they hang upside down from a branch and go to sleep.

Bushbabies sleep in the daytime in their nests of leaves. At night they look for insects, small birds and fruit to eat. They have huge, round eyes to help them see in the dark.

Animals of Australia

wallaby

kangaroo

wombat

platypus

kookaburra

koala

echidna

87

Animal families of Australia

koala

dingo

kangaroo

cuscus

budgerigar

mallee fowl

platypus

89

Koalas and mallee fowls

A koala mother has one tiny baby at a time. The baby lives in her pouch until it is six months old. Then it climbs out onto her back. She carries it there until it is almost fully grown. Sometimes the baby koala falls off. Then it cries just like a human baby until it is safely back again.

The mallee fowl lays its eggs in a very special way.
First the father bird builds a huge pile of leaves and
sand. Then he makes a hole in the top of the pile.
The mother bird lays about twenty eggs in this
hole. The leaves and sand keep the eggs warm.
If the pile gets too cold, the father adds more sand.
If it gets too hot, he takes some sand away.

When the chicks hatch,
they climb out of the pile on their own.

Animal families of tropical seashores

frigate bird

green turtle

red-footed booby

iguana

fiddler crab

flying fish

93

Green turtles and frigate birds

Green turtles spend most of their lives in the sea. When it is time to lay their eggs, mother turtles crawl out of the sea and onto the beach.

Each mother turtle digs a deep hole in the sand. There she lays about 100 eggs. She covers them with loose sand, then goes back to the sea.

In the middle of the night about ten weeks later, tiny turtles hatch from the eggs. They run quickly to the sea and swim away.

The mother frigate bird is black and white all over her body, but the father has a red throat. When the father wants to find a partner, he puffs up his throat until it is very big. The mother bird likes his big, bright throat and comes to live with him. Mother frigate birds lay one egg. Then the parents sit on it in turn until it hatches.